TEN MINU
WEATHE

LEONIE CHARLTON

Cinnamon Press
:: small miracles from distinctive voices ::

Published by Cinnamon Press
www.cinnamonpress.com
Office 49019, PO Box 92, Cardiff, CF11 1NB

Acknowledgements

Sincere thanks to the editors of *Northwords Now* for publishing 'Lapwing Central', 'Ten Minutes of Weather Away', 'Heavy Weather' and 'The Oak on Allt Coire Mhàrtuin'. Thank you to the chapbook team at The Scottish Writers' Centre for publishing 'Getting Away From the Overtalker in Iona Hostel'. Thanks also to the editors of *Anti-Heroin Chic* for publishing 'To my Body', *Gutter Voices* for publishing 'A Dream', *Dreich* for publishing 'The Weight of Bees', 'Bike', 'Sick Bed', 'Frying Pan' and 'A Raw Wind on Iona'. Thanks also to *The Blue Nib* for publishing 'Loch Etive' and 'Hogmanay'. I am indebted to Roselle Angwin for her poetry courses, Islands of the Heart and Tongues in Trees, which planted the seeds of many of these poems. Also heartfelt thanks to Em Strang and her Embodied Poetry courses, and to Chris Powici who so generously opened the world of writing poetry to me. Finally sincere thanks to the wonder that is Cinnamon Press, and to Dr Jan Fortune for her warmth, enthusiasm and keen editing eye.

Contents

Ten Minutes of Weather Away

Ten Minutes of Weather Away

In your writing shed an off-white wooden sill
dimpled with fly shit and burnt matches
balances a window pane, a jar, an eagle

feather as wide as your fist
that a man from twenty-four years ago
gave you just the other day

early sunshine takes all that in

through spiders' webs which
seem crystalline with time, yet
if you brush them with the back of your hand they'll disappear

you know that because you did it just the other day
on that other wooden sill, in that bothy
ten minutes of weather away from here

and they resolved to nothing, absolutely nothing

around a cassette tape —
Bob Dylan's *Freewheelin*
that hadn't been played in decades.

This morning, out beyond the feather and fly-shit
you see something akin to cloud-shadow
move across Ben Cruachan, graceful as a Goldie

and you have the human-most luxury
of wondering
how time might dissolve on the tongue.

I married a holly tree

on the eastern shore,
seduced by dark greenery and intensity,
roots' slowest sundering of rock,
angles of pleasure in granite thighs.
I was drawn to his moss-ridden silver,
low-down smile, muscular reach of patience.

What if, instead, I'd married his sister,
she signalling to seals from her cliff,
thriving in the lee of high stone
on a stroke of lichen and luck,
polished by weather and Blackface sheep,
watching sun fall from ravens' tongues.

How would it be to take the slight of her wind-turned wrist in my hand,
fold in to her lanolin-scented hold, feel her spines distress my hair.

Heavy Weather

For Shuna

There's a poem agitating on the B road to Abriachan.
I keep going back to where I was pulled up by a roe buck
colour of rust, the dead hare where I let the car rest.

I left the tunes on, danced on tarmac to Frazy Ford in close horse-breath air,
there in the middle of a moor of bog myrtle and pine, heather in bloom,
birch on shine, asphodel horizons of dirty gold.

Juniper bushes canted away from me in a conspiracy.
I picked the single black berry from an unready of green,
held it electric between forefinger and thumb   stopped dancing.

The hare's hips were snapped and haunches laid flat,
blood pooling to puce. Her ears rimmed in moon-sharp memory.
Front legs lifted, ready to run across the hopelessness of heather.

I pressed my thumb nail hard into the juniper berry,
breathed back to that day in May,
in the Birkwoods of Braemar, when you invited me to sit with you,

rest the horses.
I'd ridden on without a word,
through in-between worlds of juniper and wood anenome.

At my feet, on the B road To Abriachan, whiskers moved
still looking for meaning in the whickering wind.
Tears lifting for you and me, for that crushed moment.

For this hare in two halves.

A Trip to the Alder Wood in April

Alder trees yoked to the River Kinglass, you follow their steps till they solve into a bivalve of woodland. You are a stray in a shadowy place where water and eyes meet, where Holly marries Alder and Alder marries Birch, and Alder rubs Alder, rubs Alder, rubs Alder. Fans of burns count stones and from rust-dark crowns Hooded Crows harangue sweethearts

and everything is wet and wettest. You can see how these trees thrill from storm and silt, have a different way of thinking, out of the bog. How they steep this place in something that draws old hinds in to die, and other creatures to lie low in the mire for a while, and people's passions to rise among buds opaque as death.

The Weight of Bees

Bear is up on her back legs. She has woken strong. She is still furious but she's upright now, and very. Her femurs are long, like a horse's. Her lover once admired her thighs, told her they were firm and full just like the thoroughbreds they'd both ridden in past lives. Bear is glad to be up on her back legs again. Recently she's been felled over and over by her own need (the most unbearlike need) for reassurances from her lover. A bear with bloodied knees and broken leaves on her nose is not a pretty sight. She is up now and reaches past hawthorn spines to pink-dusted stigmas. She sees in this thin light that her rage is all for herself, who else when it was she who chose not to piss boundaries on the trees. Luckily she has magic in her paws, with a smudge of pollen can turn lovers into others. Hawthorn claws rend her fur as she stretches through. The blossom is barely beginning yet smells of things finishing. Bear sits down under the sudden weight of bees.

A Dream

The sheep on the hillside are pouring in from all directions, meeting along fence lines, milling between gateposts, wool wedging tight.

The hillside becomes a building, sandstone block-work some stories high. Through the windows the sheep have turned to polecats, innumerable and unutterably silent beyond glass.

They are not playing as I first thought they were. They are desperate to find a way out. Tight along they run, more and more throng to every sill, begin to spill out onto the pavement below. They stream across the street to my feet. They smell strongly of honey and fear, come to moil and musk against my cold-bone ankles. It's something chemical they're running from. I cannot help them, I am as scared as they are. I don't even have the scent of honey to redeem me.

Stormbound on Eigg

Buffeted. You are beating it along the escarpment above Cleadale, past the Finger of God and smoke-signalling waterfalls. Storm Ciara growing your strides to match the powerful warrior women they say once roamed this island. Eilean nam Ban Mòra. Your life, slow tilt of this ridge, a summonsing between light and dark, a call to stay with each deep and blistering moment.

Questions of balance in storm-bound days. Calmac's MV Lochnevis berthed in Mallaig and hail stones stinging your skin. Your feet flexing over curves of spheroidal erosion on the shore, toes widening among swum-memories of Hugh Miller's plesiosaurs. Storm-starlings flicker in gusts, gulls and crows lift up and fall back over and over in the roar. Only seals and ravens hold their own.

Sea foam blows past like salted butterflies of the full Snow Moon. Laig Bay a bivalve holding you in the eye of the storm, capacities of presence all around in this geology, in your body, in that oystercatcher hunkering down around her shadow on the wet steely sand. All of this in thrall to Rum, where *his* blood runs from, dark precious pony who has taught you to be occasionally, solidly, present.

Back up on that ridge, on your own two feet, high winds hone your surrender as you head towards the shoulder of your some-day death. You think about falling onto your knees, even as you veer west down the zigzag path through wind-groomed heather, in the lean of a powerful woman's skyline-brows and nose and breasts, down past two bony and watchful horses, back to the beach, to the basalt shelves, the reptilian languor that reminds you to be here, amid gravity, mid-flow in your longing towards Rum, its Cuilins, badass and beautiful and silver-happed.

A Raw Wind on Iona

Through the window a flock
of peat-woolled Hebrideans
grazes above a teal sea.
Unhurried horns all face North.

I step outside the hostel to find a day
that has gaeled the birds away,
a morning to fold into, and over,
with all the heart-heft I can muster.

Getting Away from the Overtalker in Iona Hostel

Freezing sward scours my feet
morning air cools my tea
in the too thick mug far too quickly.

Big bare sun lifting over Mull glares my eyes
burns the starlings' chatter to sound-silhouettes
raises the fenceline to a diatribe.

And the geese roughly tell it how it *really* is
and a single brilliant gannet courses the horizon
and the whole while skylarks are cooking up the blue

and I love, just love, how lapwings change their minds in mid air.

Thresholds on Iona

Just a couple of things, the tall American said to the warden outside the hostel. *If I take my shoes off I can't walk, so is it okay if I keep them on inside?* My eyes skipped his shorts, slid down his prosthetic shins.

He lost his legs in Somalia, twenty-six years ago, in a land mine explosion. He's at a threshold in his life, he tells me, he has found God but his wife hasn't.

Could the sky be any bluer? He asks, looking up, his voice cracked with rescue. Then he sets off.

I walk barefoot to Traigh-na-Criche. Keep a vague eye out for the American's listing stride, but it's just me on the machair. The tide is out and the sand is hard. My feet resent the weight of me. I am looking for pistachio seams of epidote, they say it helps with negative judgment. I leave the beach, stepping over mandates of bird tracks. I choose that moment, that precise moment, to turn my head towards Dun I. A male hen harrier flies the same route, his black wingtips, the jolt of his bullet profile, lay me down. When I wake I am thick with calm. I flex my ten toes. The air above my head changes shape, him, again, harrying the sandy threshold between machair and marram. Could he be any closer? Could the sky be any bluer?

Lapwing Central

Between Balevullin and Balinoe, by shallow ponds and fallen stones, lapwings lift into the air, taking me with them on each beatific beat, scooping me clean with rounded wings, giggling me silly with rubber-soled squeaks, taking my breath away with somersaults and spins till I'm high, high amongst the torn clouds, amongst falling feathers, latching onto their drifts and kinks till I'm down on all fours by the un-standing stone, palms pressed against the tightly-cropped turf, fingers pointing to feathers lying askance, each one glanced by lines splitting loam-brown from sea-foam white, each one folding my vertebrae bit by bit till my eyes are level with the daisies and buttercups and tiny balls of sheep dung, till I'm spooning with the stone, pressing back into its lichen-lipped embrace, breathing in the lanolin-and-clover scent of summer at its zenith, and feeling as ready as I ever will for the 18:55 Calmac to Oban.

Hazel

In this toe-hold of hill
rockspilt water
croons to oak, craze of rose

hazel tree, one of three—
sweet snakescrib of silvers
holding my thirsty gravity

among ribs of trust
reaching to a sky of milknuts.
Here, everything inclines upwards

—even the falling water
is broken by the light.

Winter Birchwoods

From bed he looks outside
the burgundy is back

she turns to the hillside
her eyes, slow to line up with his
see that autumn is already past

the night wind has stripped
the birch branches bare
has left them outstanding

tears ease down her face
slow as sap

Time

For twenty-one years he's baked bread
cleaned his farmer's hands on raw dough
kneaded with hacked knuckles, let rise, let fall

now he's stopped, to do with ketogenesis
while his body reduces, firms up to that of another,
she wonders whether

they'll see out another seven-year cycle, let alone three,
you see, so much depends on the rise and fall
and on clean hands, or at least the possibility.

Frying Pan

Amongst chanterelle
birch leaves glitter

you burn fingers picking them out
I want to plate them in gold

for the sake of forever.

You break a hard-shelled egg
one feather fascinated to its side

breakfast   too beautiful to bear.

The Oak on Allt Coire Mhàrtuin

A crumple of hill hides
The Tanning Pool, eye
of Kyloe-dark dreaming:

leather steeping, bellows
fanning Ardmaddy Furnace
for pig iron and warfare.

Above this watchful place
two copper-pink hinds, hefted here
break like peace into bracken

high ears lift away, flick back
on the weight of your breath,
an invitation to get wind of the day

for you the chances are slim.
You head for an oak reigning
over helter of the rising burn.

Up close, ferns and flying rowans
trust with fragile roots
from the hollow of its throat.

The oak shouts for nothing.
You stack vertebrae 'round its deep belly,
it takes your back

more completely than bone can believe.
Turning your face to barksin
you lose your lips in shadow

ache to be rewritten in oak gall ink
each sepal of your lungs, bough of your mind
defined, indelibly

note the rhythm of my charcoal chambers
ink me viable,
please, you whisper, your mouth full of moss.

Apple Trees at Ardmaddy

It has been said that Kazakhstan's two gifts to the world are the cultivated apple and the tamed horse. Last summer, loosed in the little orchard at Ardmaddy, two Spanish-blooded horses were driven demented by midges. We passed on tea with Alasdair and legged it, girths untightened, gear all a-guddle.

A year and a ripening later the gate to the orchard is left open for the deer family—a hind, her calf, and last year's offspring, the knobber. They tread lightly, these three, just heavily enough to stir the ground with slots, to leave their mark though the narrow leaning wire-mesh gate. Alasdair is glad to have the windfall applies eaten, the grass kept down. Most of all he is glad of the trodden path. Somebody's mother planted the trees, he remembers. I watch from a distance, tea in hand, swipe winged deer ticks off my face as pipistrelles spill and an eleven-pointer roars. Eat your fill, mild-eyed yearling, soon enough you will be pushed away by strutting stags. For now stay in close, the apples are abundant, your mother still tends you. Down by the loch, within earshot, four ringed plovers are holding back the tide.

Bike

Darling, don't be a bike,
Mum said to me on the phone
a long time ago

I was going on a date
with a good man
but that's by the by.

Six syllables spilling over me as I walk upriver
against rain, trace a white-throated dipper
drowning itself in torrents of wind

wet rock raises lichen into fierce relief, Mum's colours:
peacock, russet, gold, oxidised blood. She's been dead
a decade, the river is coming on strong, I hunker down

by the pool they call The Pot where sea trout leap in summer
sheer silhouettes of muscle and drive
today my eyes are lost in white miasma

veils of rock-spun water hiding the secrets between
that could sink you to sick
turn you pure snow-melt green

to be water-flung
spittle and spit and spawn
to be fallen.

What had mattered was the sting in the *darling.*

Hold Me There

They fold my knees like a tomahawk

two breast feathers, barn owl
spooning on the bog myrtle, allowing
the breeze to move their vanes

with aching shins I straighten

away from that restive intimacy
hope for catkins in bud, my own height
to snag my hair, just hold me there.

The Cure

'We used to call him tip-toe cos he couldn't bend his knees, on account of the emphysema, no, the skin thing, eczema, aye. His knees were all cracked, the skin at the back of them. One day we were skiing at Glenshee, he fell in a hole of sphagnum moss, fucking cured him didn't it. Came back though.'

'You've so many stories.'

'Aye, like the peat I am, some storage. When you're fed up of listening to me though, you're not to cut me into squares and burn me on the fire, or stack me into a wee tippy outside... You know, Scotland and Russia, the only places in the world with peat this deep.'

To my Body

A gathering of earthy deposits
I would sit here
among your many river-stone selves
watching your personal shift
of cartilage on granite on moss

I know now the worn unlovedness of you
the tearstruck slick of you
how the quartz in your heart glitters and scars

I touch the perfection of your unholy edges
capture how your mind has cauterised
till you spill to the spaces between

I lift up through the compressed weight of you
I fall into cave-dark love with you

Sick Bed

Screeds of hail pulse past your window
cross the Cowpark among hoodies all-a-spin
the sea eagle drawls in
to pig guts left out on the knoll

and you in bed—slowly, poorly, you
too ill you say to be up and about
but well enough to watch the storm
to lay warm fingers on yourself,

find a skudding swell that takes you deep
somewhere unaccountable and dark
beyond hail and mind and pig-death.

Renovating the Bothy

He told me, tape measure in hand,
how when he lived there—some thirty years ago
there was no wood burner   fuck all

and the head keeper controlled the generator
so when he decided it was lights out
that was it   everyone went to bed.

Stepping over bare joists
I feel its panting—
a robin trapped
in dark-webbed corner

I go to open the stuck window
shove the lever, glass starts sliding
—not enough belief in my fingers
to stem the fall

single pane rains down
past *Freewheelin* cassette still on the sill
past swerve of flaking tup's horn
past sun-bashed curtains

air rushes in
robin rushes out

and me
I just stay
with this fluttering breath.

Hogmanay

Snowing hard in Aviemore when you met the train
me getting warm on the bench-seat of a Land Rover
you liking my jumper, all I remember a storm of colour

pulled-over kisses on a blizzardy bend, your Mum and Dad,
their hearts embering in a dark house — *her* sense of humour
on-target like yours, that slow-roast wild goose

like nothing I'd tasted before, or since.
I remember a lot of sex, drams, dancing
I remember snow-drifts, trees bending under white weight.

One morning branches let go of snow, sprang up,
your phone rang, I saw you slip felt you go.

I put myself on the Edinburgh train
(feistiness I admire in my younger self)
not waiting for you to come back

from that phone-call outpost
where you'd blurred
while I'd burned.

Trains and East Coast consonants,
Caledonian pines   wild geese   you   the past
all still get to me when heavy snow's forecast.

In a Time of No Hugs

For years their velvet nostrils have flickered
simple whickers at the sight of each other

silver-grey horses, two wings of the same moth.

In this cold March wind chunks of white hair tilt by
as the vet gently trims where veins must lie

they go down quickly
her pulse beats longer than his

until they are stilled
bright bodies in a final alignment

no sign of the melanoma that was killing them
no traffic passing on the Corona-quiet road,

the herd stands in a soundless arc
only your sobs break this rain into pieces.

The Mare's Tail Waterfall on Beinn nan Aighenan

The Mare's Tail
felting rock
true whale-blue

Mare's Tail
fated love
on the move

Mare's Tail
culmination
of backbone

Mare's Tail
stealing granite's
thunder

Mare's Tail
lowering you
lonely

Mare's Tail
bump starting
breach of tears

Mare's Tail
staunching
guilt

Mare's Tail
gauging
gravitas

Mare's Tail
winnowing
spilt hope

Mare's Tail
carrying on
regardless

Loch Etive

I remember the bad stuff

but today it's sun
and seal breath

green hairstreak butterflies
mind-blowing on gorse.

www.ingramcontent.com/pod-product-compliance
Ingram Content Group UK Ltd.
Pitfield, Milton Keynes, MK11 3LW, UK
UKHW032125030325
4838UKWH00004B/269

9 781788 640749